THE HEART IS AN UNDERTAKER BEE

Brice Maiurro

The Heart is an Undertaker Bee
©2023, Brice Maiurro

No part of this book may be reproduced by any means known at this time or derived henceforth without written permission of the publisher or author. The exception would be in the case of brief quotations embodied in the critical articles or reviews and pages where permission is specifically granted by the publisher or author.

Books may be purchased in quantity and/or special sales by contacting the publisher. All inquiries related to such matters should be addressed to:

Middle Creek Publishing & Audio
9161 Pueblo Mountain Park Road
Beulah, CO 81023

editor@middlecreekpublishing.com

(719) 369-9050

First Paperback Edition, 2023
ISBN: 978-1-957483-14-6

Front Cover Art: Vincent Cheap

Author Image: J. Mark Tebben

Printed in the United States

Praise for *The Heart is an Undertaker Bee*

"Brice Maiurro shares the truths one can find if one looks closely. In The Heart is an Undertaker Bee, nature is venerated. Each voice is soft, gentle, respectful, and humble. These poems do not exploit nature as a subject. They acknowledge our place within the living world, "We are still under the tree,/ beneath the everything." There is wisdom in these poems, like the saguaros who "…hold their arms/ straight up towards/ the open sky—/ sur-render/ in reverence/ to one/ another.""

—Huascar Medina,
 Kansas Poet Laureate Emeritus, author of Un Mango Grows in Kansas

"It is truly astonishing that a man who co-created an open mic named Punketry and led millions of people in organized howling could write poetry that is so good at capturing the quiet moments. Brice Maiurro's new collection is a testament to a life spent listening, sitting with the disaster while trying to make sense of it, it is a still pond reflecting back a forest fire. A sometimes-manic book filled with inconsiderate pop stars, countless trees, the occasional ghost, Congress Park and Colfax, talking animals, unanswerable questions, astral projection, ambitious flowers, dirt, hope, grief, and most importantly and undeniably—love. Not that generic love, the good honest blue-collar stuff. It's good poetry for the people, and it makes Denver Poetry proud."

—Ken Arkind,
 author of *Coyotes* and *Denver*

""I'm just so happy to see something alive," Maiurro writes, narrowly breaking the fourth wall as I read this collection, thinking the same. Black Mountain and Jack Spicer would be proud."

—Barracuda Guarisco,
 author of *It's Not a Lie If You Believe It* (Voice Lux Press)

"Brice Maiurro's new collection, The Heart Is An Undertaker Bee, is an encapsulation of escapable moments through this mortal coil, and a return on togetherness as loss. Maiurro gives us a mirror as words to enter a tangling place of living as long as trees extend their branches reaching high always dancing. There is the remembrance, the *quaking, the sound of the bang, the music, the choir of hands*, bringing us to *an echo of sound* and of motion, an instance that places us in each of these poems. The shapes of things that make these poems tether through time and age to remember the womb of the world.

—Crisosto Apache,
   author of *Ghostword* (Gnashing Teeth Publishing)

"These poems create a body that laughs, buries, bargains, climbs, and *chews on life like candy*. You will taste the sweetness and feel the crackle of a cellophane wrapper around your own limbs as a wrapped tree, teaching you, again, how to worship into the *swollen heart of the moment*. This volume is *a return to what is real, what matters,* and a journey of joy!"

—Valerie A. Szarek,
   Poet, Teacher, Shamanic Practitioner, author of *Offerings, Soar Ready: Medicine Poems for a Changing World, Signs of Life*

""Take care of your grief," poet Brice Maiurro thoughtfully tells the reader towards the end of his fourth poetry collection *The Heart is An Undertaker Bee*. By that point the poet has explored the relationship between interior and exterior life, humanity's relationship with nature (from trees, lakes, cacti, and "mountains named after terrible men"), human beings' relationships with one another (of particular note is the moving love poem "Under the Tree, Beneath the Everything), and human days being boxed onto calendars. In this vivid collection, Maiurro explores many poetic forms and dimensions of human experience. His vulnerability to walk both up and down the stairs within himself (see "Sound Reverberated Off of Mountains") and share what he finds is inspiration for us all to be brave enough to keep on living and take care of ourselves (and each other) along the way."

—Cristina A. Bejan,
   author of the Award-Winning *Green Horses on the Walls*

THE HEART IS AN UNDERTAKER BEE

Brice Maiurro

Middle Creek Publishing & Audio
Beulah, CO   USA

TABLE OF CONTENTS

9 | A Letter to the Office of Death
11 | Anatomy of a 34-Year-Old Man
13 | Bon Iver is my Roommate
14 | I Am Waiting for the War to End
15 | Meditation on Trees
17 | Dishwasher Haiku
18 | I Have Been Tending a Digital Garden
19 | The Lake
20 | Roundabout
21 | Shelsea said,
22 | A Tree in Congress Park
24 | I See You There in Half Lotus
30 | Volver
32 | Swimming Lessons
33 | Bisonte
34 | Bravery
35 | Mathematics
37 | Sound Reverberated Off of Mountains
40 | Pome
42 | The Night Shift
43 | Owlhead
45 | Chicken Soup for the Dark Night of the Soul
47 | Walking Into the Forest at Night
49 | Nocturne No. 1 in D-Flat Major
51 | (Milkweed) Song
52 | Fishing
55 | The Stand Off
57 | Under the Tree, Beneath the Everything
59 | Catalog of Flowers
62 | How to Make a Lake
65 | Not

67 | On Grief
69 | New Horse
70 | Involution

75 | *Acknowledgements*
77 | *About the Author*

These poems exist somewhere
between a city and a mountain.

A LETTER TO THE OFFICE OF DEATH

I am no farmer,
and I have
never carried
a sickle.

A blade
pulled across wheat
is as foreign to me
as taking a sick dog
and a shotgun
far enough into a field
where the children
will certainly hear the bang
but not the whimper.

I have never pulled
a barely breathing fox
out of the wrapped carnage
of the mangling of
a barbed-wire trap.

I have never
killed the fox
to save my hens.

I have never
killed my hens
to feed my children.

My farm
is a silent caricature

slapped on the plastic label
of a neatly frozen fragment

far from the spaceless cage
where the soul of the creature
once died.

Death is no longer
any kind of reaper.

I write to you
a request
to cease and desist
from this portrait of death
as the reaper
he no longer is.

Death no longer pulls life
from the ground
with his calloused hands.

The death
that we know best
is four walls containing
a perfect climate
and a music that is
whatever we need it to be

to cover the sound of the bang,
as well as the whimper.

ANATOMY OF
A 34-YEAR-OLD-MAN

A forest of giant redwood trees.

Neck craning up
because after all—
the question at the beginning
tends to be
where does it all end?

Stepping softly
through this parliament of trees,
a quiet so quiet
there is ample space to feed
even the hungriest of thoughts.

Tree after tree
what we've stepped into
is a brotherhood,

a silent choir,
an old story,
figuring out
how to tell itself.

There in the graceful wilderness,
where the ferns learned to thrive
within the shadow of time,
is a white tree,
no less tall than the others,
no less wide than the others,
shining with a magic

that cannot be anything
but embraced.

Shining like it caught sight
of the moon itself and wanted
nothing more than to become it.

I look
in the mirror
each morning
at the single white hair
in the vast forest of trees
that frame the edges
of my face,
and I know
that there it will stay,

my own little microcosm
of moon,

my reminder of magic,

curved like a question mark
at the end of the sentence—
where does it all end?

BON IVER IS MY ROOMMATE

Bon Iver never offers to pay for my Del Taco.

Bon Iver is chronically late to racquetball.

Bon Iver leaves the pots in the sink to soak
    but he never finishes rinsing them out.

Bon Iver sets like seven alarms in the morning.

Bon Iver bought these cowboy boots
    after binge-watching a ton of Sergio Leone
    movies one weekend
    and he never wears them.

Bon Iver always puts on the Meat Puppets
    when he's high on edibles.

Bon Iver has nothing but posters of Van Gogh paintings
    up on the walls of his room.

Bon Iver buys a few sticks of Speed Stick at a time
    so he doesn't have to buy Speed Stick so often,

and Bon Iver goes through these really somber winters
where he'll just disappear into the woods for days on end
and no one will hear from him and he'll come back
and disappear into his room for a short eternity,

and he'll come out with these beautiful songs
and they're really good.

Sometimes they're really good.

I AM WAITING FOR THE WAR TO END

The war never left Hiroo Onoda,

Japanese soldier
forever on an island.

In the autumn of the war
they dropped leaflets from planes
singing it's over, it's over,
but the war never left for him.

They gave him a war
and then he was the war,
and home never came for him.

I am waiting for the war to end.

Above my head
they drop the leaflets
and all around me
are victory songs
sung by dead singers.

We set fire to our jungle,
and all of our wilderness
that we abandoned there.

The war is our cave now,
our last meal every meal,
the war is our mother.

As softly as a tree
on an island on fire,
I am waiting for the war to end.

MEDITATION ON TREES

So there are these trees and frankly these trees should be everywhere. I open my mouth–I want trees to come pouring forth from the very back of my throat. I want trees in clouds in the sky as my shoes root to the Earth like clutching a lover's hand in dangerous times. Somewhere there's a factory that once made trees that has since been shut down. Somewhere there are voices in the soil begging for revival, for justice, for love, love like trees. How sad to pass by trees so fast, at 45 miles per hour, alone on roads that once held trees. I wanna see the trees. To march right up to them like elders on an earthen throne and say I see you. I see you, trees. You, which breathe in tandem with me. You, which die at the hands of greed, set aflame by momentary gain as everything, including these fleeting thoughts begin to dissolve around me. Love me like the sun, the rivers, the mountains looming like the most patient meditation. Love me how I deserve to be loved. Kiss me like tectonic plates crashing together. Like trees entangled, trees that have grown so long and now in time intertwine, shaking away that idea of being separate. Trees like a music, different stories in one sound. Let us not be trees resigned to medians. Singular trees captured by highways. Let us be trees that hold sound like secrets and let it fill us brimming with light. A tree that calls to you. For miles, you travel unaware and accompanied by grace. You find your way through the dark night to the wanton alter of a lone tree that against all odds blooms in season, there in the dead of the night desert. The tree that was never expected. Elsewhere, a tree grows in the nutrients of death around it. Elsewhere, trees grow on the south side of this planet completely unaware as they reach up to the sky, that they grow upside down, gravity pulling and pulling them in, keeping them close to where they have come from to arrive in each moment and the moment thereafter. I wish to arrive the same way. Brave enough to live and continue to live. I wish to move with the wind though still rooted. These trees are constant as time. These trees hold stories in rings that were never meant to be worn around the flesh of fingers. I run into the wilderness flooded by the thicket of life surrounding me and placing my hand to the heartbeat of a tree, waters running upwards in defiance of everything.

DISHWASHER HAIKU

Beneath the Zen music,
I couldn't hear the rivers
in the dishwasher.

I HAVE BEEN TENDING A DIGITAL GARDEN

I have been tending a digital garden,
growing eight-bit beets
deep in the roots of the pixelation,
and when my avatar chews the sweet blood
from their electric life,
my mouth is baptized in the same juice.

In the warm wake of this digital morning,
I awoke to a square-eyed crow,
eating at the plot of me,
its mouth red-forty red,
I sang to him it's okay and
it's okay,

I'm just so happy to see something
alive.

THE LAKE

      I explained to you
                about the lake,
        how if you went in,
                you'd be overcome by a feeling

        of a melancholy
                that never truly ends.
      It stays with you forever,
                like a scar across the amygdala.

You dipped your toes in
              and your toes made way for the rest of you.
              You looked at me,

        fully immersed in the cold water and said,
                does it really feel any different,
all of that lake you're carrying inside of you?

ROUNDABOUT

After Khadija Queen

this is my roundabout way of saying	the squares of your calendar rounds at the edges	and heaven, if anything, knows defiance
the ghost of a dying forest is screaming at you from the other side	perhaps you haven't been born yet	perhaps you're dying to get there
that's all, that's all, that's all	the paper—furling like fingers into fists	we're best left inside and listening for the curve

SHELSEA SAID,

    this is amazing;
    it is raining right now and
    you can't even tell.

A TREE IN CONGRESS PARK

Squints and I had taken a solid dose
of wilderness and managed to navigate
the madness to sail our ships to Congress
Park. Whatever you call that punch of blue
that slips in right before the golden hour
departs. We chewed on life like candy.
We were greeted by a tree.

She had limbs like elders have stories.
She held moonlight like she was balancing
several cups of chamomile in her open arms.

She prayed how I wish I prayed. In every
moment. The grass was starting to swallow
Squints. I pulled him up and out of the verdant
void. His eyes returned jetlagged and fanfare.

My open palm asked the tree if I could climb her.
She pulled me up in turn, up and out of that same
growing verdant void and I spoke bear in my body,
climbing like fire to the top of that tree, peaking
up and out at the curved Earth. Then came the echo—
Squints below, hollering a no but I hollered back
permission! I hollered the permission the tree had
taught me. Limbs like stories, a million cups of
chamomile balanced in her promise to hold us.

The holler was received. He climbed baby bear
up and into the swollen heart of this moment.
Scratched tattoo by the queer branches bending.
Night. We saw only silence. Squint's heart was
a pitter-patter and I was waiting, and then he
arrived. We were tall as magic. Knee-deep in
death but our heads inseparable from the clouds.

The wind was sober and dancing with us. The moon was the moon. The sky was singing and Squints, I love you. You gift. You gift of taking my hand, when nothing was logic and the sky was poetry, but not the kind that flows out of the cup but the kind you have to fight for.

We climbed. Up and out of the verdant void to be tall as this tree dreamed of for you and I, Squints.

Eternal. Dying. Tall.

I SEE YOU THERE
IN HALF LOTUS

eating the flowers off of the wallpaper,

        carving circles into Persian rugs,

                mind pacing back and forth
                        across the shadow
                            of a metronome.

                    I too have slept on the
          blade of a fingernail moon,

awoken on fire like the sun,

        I live in that same mirror that you look into.

                I see you there in half lotus,

      mourning the death in the chicken scratch

              ledgers of your doctors,

recapping the taste of the hook that never left your mouth,

      parading through your own garden

              for an audience of your own mice,

swimming through the air six feet above the ground,

    entangled in joy,

        in vegan joy,

I see you there in half lotus,

            floating on the backside of the water,

        pacing in your concrete block shoes,

    waxing your wooden wings,

I am barely a poet except in the same sense we all are.

I am in love with you, each day, dear day, dear solstice,

        dear reimagined wooden reality,

          carved in pirouette,

    petrified in the sixth chamber of a Russian revolver,

I see you there in half lotus,

half dead,   half reborn,   half unborn,   half stillborn,

fully,
    fully,
        fully   alive.

I dot the paths you walk across with invisible ink,

and a keen sense of optimism

about the future,

your future,

our collective future,

the future   we share,

as we share half a communion wafer and stay seated,

laughing at the priest.

I find myself sleeping in the echoes of the

church of my everyday baptism,

wherein I re-remember from the past life of
yesterday how I best loved myself.

How I cared for my carriage

as to chariot you through coliseums.

All of you,

I dare you to eat an entire barrel of peaches.

I dare you to see what I think I see:

that pleasure exists in single frames void of pain,

that there is a moment

when we are as golden

as we'll ever be,

that our green days are only less because they are more,

                              counting is a failed system.

I see you there still in half lotus.

I see you there still in cosmic dissonance.

I see you there still a whole mother,

a wonderful mother to this poem.

                A beautiful death to the person I wasn't.

                My funeral will just be a bunch of me's

            laughing and laughing,

confusedly asking ourselves who died?

                        Don't be a marcescent tree.

            Fall asleep in the movie

            (you're still experiencing it.)

I will cradle you in the maternity ward of my most favorite memories.

I will laugh at how dumb you were, we were, we are.

I will never let death, or television, or morning commutes allow me to forget that I miss you.

I channel frustration out onto a byzantine scroll the length of my contract this time through.

I sincerely apologize to my editors for how much honesty they'll have to edit out.

    I see you there in front of deep thick miles of green forest
and I'm begging you you're facing the wrong way turn around,

        turn around,

                turn around,

                        hey look, now we're dancing.

        I cannot tell you how much I love
        the way you dance around a fire.

Every single generation of your ancestors
would be so proud.

        You wave me into the sky with your clipped wings.

        I'm trying to tell you I'm traveling already.

        I'm trying to tell you there is literally no rush,
        there will always be a next bus.

I'm trying to say a lot of truly preposterous things,

and I stand behind all of them.

                Let's go dancing,

in half lotus,   all maroon,

        the bebop   of drunk   misstep   sober as our love.

                      We're not two halves,

                we're not complete bagels either.

                There are holes in the center.

    That's intentional—

        that's where the wind travels through.

        That's where we pick back up.

              We don't find ourselves where
              we left ourselves.

We leave them there

to puppy love

or to be Margot and Jack,

        bickering for fucking fun.

We leave them there to us

    laughing and crying.

              We wax and we wane.

        In some moments we disappear,

              only to come back as flowers,

        perennials each and every year.

I see you there in half lotus,

echoing in those cathedrals

which we've left as we found them.

I see you there in half lotus,

rainwater soaking the heart side of your rib cage.

There is nothing to fear.

We all want to drown in the right kinds of love.

VOLVER

We used to dance here

We used to take our government chips out
here

Let our wilderness off its leash and run rampant
with it through the forest

We used to hang legs from tree branches
worship Upside-Down Mountain
and birds that dove upward

We used to pack the snow in
with our thrift store boots
and hand-me-down jackets

Past the threshold of town
we were free to be children
gathering sticks to make our own homes
our own skylit ceilings
our own cradle to crawl into

Time crawled into running
the world unlearned how to turn
so slowly and me left craving
this place this quake
this eggshell cracking open
of the smoky bottle of my spirit
so I returned

greeted by no children no new epiphany
no ghost the ghosts were gone too

our homes built up of gathered sticks
had fallen

the wilderness had followed
us out

and into the boxes of tomorrow's
calendar

I was no longer there
either

it seems I had returned to remember
why I had left in the first place

SWIMMING LESSONS

                        You become a rowboat
and the lake finds its way to you.
                  You become a canoe
and you find yourself a river,
    and you stumble down eternal
        into sure doom and dangerous love,
through all the ugly trees that threaten
    the sky you think you own,
        and as sudden as a slow dance,
                  you become a raft
      splayed out across an ocean
      surrounding you,
like a womb
        —sorry,
                I meant tomb.

BISONTE

      oh yes   yes you do
    my lovely love my   wind–song
stormstress painted   lily death defying
morning   star kiss   me   something
   ragged & kiss me fresh out of the
magic fog   of the hot   shower & I will
kiss   you   oh yes yes you
   my love today my love yesteryear   oh
my all tomorrow's parties   &
   so why not why not   more
   I realign to   you &   I bend
      around you my branches   open
         towards the open   mouth
  of   life   &   love   &
      I write you   poems inside of
    my poems &   the poems
    write themselves   in my
  sleep where I   keep
in my sweet   little   safe
  a   picture   of   you & I
  beneath the eiffel tower
  which no one   needs to
    know is   just the
   transmission tower
      that holds
      the power lines
    right   off of
   the busy boulevard
   in the part of town where
    they once
      tested the nukes
   but now   that's where
   the buffalo   roam

BRAVERY

The cactus turned to the sky and asked,
What are those white things strewn out across you?

Those are my bravery,
said the sky,
And you? Where is your
bravery?

It is here, said the cactus, *in these needles*
that come bursting forth from me.

Well,
said the sky,
that seems like a silly bravery.

No, said the cactus—
What is silly
is to spend our time together
comparing our braveries.

MATHEMATICS

    The wind swings my screen door
    like a hatchet.

                        My chest is a heavy bookcase
                        of all the books I have bought
                                but haven't read.

    SWAT car cops hang
    on each side of my brain.
    They block off the intersection
    of audacity
    and substance.

                        The wind manifests in soundless jazz.

    I bite my nails perfectly.
    My teeth dig up the dirt
    buried beneath.
    (The tiny funeral where
    I hide what I can't make
    perfect.)

                            An attempt at the velvet death
                                of unrelenting inertia.

    On the ceiling of my most intimate
    singular night,
    a mule walks toward me,
    bestowed with beautiful packs
    that carry wasted space.

                            I've named the mule after myself
                              and it begins to kick the air.

The mule and I
we dream.

Well,
we attempt to do the
math of it all.

SOUND REVERBERATED OFF OF MOUNTAINS

I swallowed the city
before the city could swallow me.

In anticipation of the haunted smog
which rolls along like mustangs
into the last open field of my America.

I watched a dream die.
A dream of big thoughts
like lightning bolts,
large and unsustainable,
filling the last pixelated square of
unlit wanderlust.

And in the unlit wanderlust
I learned to walk by sound.
I learned to move
by the layered truths of reality
and I learned to love
what I have not yet seen
but that which I truly believe
exists.

I swallowed the city
inward like two aspirin tablets
past the vacuum of the spaces
between my sweet teeth
onward in rivers to the pit of me.

I felt the brick walls falling
in the canyons of me

like sixty-seven thousand soup cans falling down
endless flights of stairs,

and inside of me there are
endless flights of stairs and
each day I ask myself if I am
going to walk downward into
them or if I am going to climb
up them and on a planet where
north is our best guess I won't
know if I'm heading south,
but only that these stairs just
keep unfolding.

The city attempted to swallow
me in its placebo fever of death
and I yelled deep, deep into the
belly of the city as to make it
bounce back against the
mountains in hopes of
disorienting the city that I loved
into possibly thinking it was and is
hearing the voice of God,

because we all are and I can't
argue with you about that of which
I am certain. That my God is a
God of sound reverberated off of
mountains and we push it right
back against it until we hear a
full-mantled chorus of every
fire and every flood in our
wet, hot lives.

The way that we
give birth is in every way.

I think about the way
we father our poems
and days and then we
let them go.

I drown in sweaty, undying brows
of om dripping with the hard work
of a soul in its best sunlight.

I still plant seeds for later.

I swallowed the city and
from my belly, the city grew.

POME

They may call you
the tree that can't grow peaches
or the tree that won't grow pears,

and you may even call yourself
the tree that loses its leaves in the fall,
or the tree in the shade of that bigger tree,

and some days you might hear
that voice calling you
the tree with the broken branch,
or the tree that isn't a mountain,
or a stream, or a trout, or a singer,
or a deer, or good at math,
but that voice
is not a divine voice.

The divine voice
is the voice that won't hear any of this,

because it is too busy dancing,
shaking your fruit to the floor of the Earth,
to share, to give, to feed,

because it is too busy singing this song,
the song you know by heart,
that sings music over any noise,
singing and singing and singing
I am an apple tree,
I am an apple tree,
I am an apple tree.

THE NIGHT SHIFT

I was restless
in bed
in the womb
of the night
and I knew
I had to
get out.

I was stuck
on sunflowers
and my distinct
lack of knowing
what they get
up to once
the sun goes
down.

I walked barefoot
into the void
and wandered
and wandered
some more
until I found
a sunflower,
sitting there
praying to
the moon

and it said to me
nothing
belongs to only
one god.

I don't know
if that means
as much to you
as me
but I'm glad
I went
and checked in

because someone
needs to keep an eye
on these things.

OWLHEAD

She tells me that now and then
she likes to put on this owlhead.

She explains to me that when she
has her owlhead on, she can see
in so many directions at once.

She says it slows her down,
being able to view the world
in such a panoramic way,
through the view of an owl.

In her day-to-day life,
she tells me, sometimes
it feels like she has
tunnel vision,

and like she only has
three minutes
for everything.

That is why I put on
the owlhead,
she tells me.

I can watch the moon
move slow at night.

I can see the field mice
below me in its glow
and grab them
in my claws,
she tells me.

But sometimes,
she tells me,
when I put on
the owlhead
I can't sleep.

I become restless—
spooked by each
and every sound.

I am consumed by it,
and I never know when
the fear will come
for me.

I tell her maybe you
shouldn't put on the owlhead.

Maybe instead just take off,
now and then,
into the forest at night.

I have tried that,
she says to me,
but there is nothing for me
that makes me feel
the way I feel
when I wear
the owlhead.

There just is nothing
that slows me down
the same way.

CHICKEN SOUP FOR THE DARK NIGHT OF THE SOUL

Drink coffee until you're manic,
manic until you're lying in your dead room,
your dead room until you realize you're never
going to sleep again.

Throw on yr shoes and hoodie and vanish
down the highway, down the highway forever
until you reach the pass, turn down the pass
blasting Fleet Foxes yapping on yr midnight
radio.

Burn through the forest like a machete,
machete yr way to the basecamp to nowhere,
know where you came from and forget it,
arrive at the base of the mountain,
welcomed by silent campers and
bystander ghosts of terrible men with mountains
named after them.

Mantra that you will make yr way up the mountain,
your rucksack full of midnight & taurine & trail mix
and traverse the bones of empty houses to the trailhead
until you realize that you drove two hours
down the midnight highway on a quarter tank of gas
to the pass to park to roam to arrive at a place where you
will never find yr way up the mountain,

so you think it's time to go home, but home is a star
and you are a strange sailor, and yr nobody but not
in the Buddhist way.

You say goodbye to maps and fire and a dream
and then your breath leaves too. You decide to
sleep where you believe you are, in the woods,
in the cold, at the big rock at the base of the
mountain,

and you blanket yr hoodie on you, and you kiss
the distant stars goodnight, and the wolves howl,
they howl like the hungriest neighbors you've ever
had and you wonder what to make of neighbors
with no fences,

you don't want to run from their teeth, or the cold,
or back to the fickle arms of the city,
so you close your eyes,
and you sleep, and tomorrow,

tomorrow you'll hold an empty promise
like the wheel of a dream traversing the dark roads
of the side of a mountain like a nightmare
named after terrible men.

WALKING INTO THE FOREST AT NIGHT

You may think it is light
that absolves the darkness
but that is not so.

Light is but our loveliest way
of deferring the truth of darkness.

You may think it wise
to try to show the darkness
that you can outdark it,
but that is not so,

for the darkness speaks
and has always spoken
with the same tongue
that lives in the deep hollow
of your mouth.

There is nothing really
but to sit with the darkness,
to listen to the pain
that exists within its shell,

that same pain
that in aching time may birth
a reverie,
or a war,
or a garden,
or a winter.

It is there
that an old language

can once again be heard
before the certain return
of the light.

The light,
where you will carry with you,
like a torch,
the darkness of you,
the darkness of everything.

NOCTURNE NO. 1
IN D-FLAT MAJOR

And one night there was a shadow outside of my window.
I unlatched the hinge and floated through
to the other side.

I floated over the brick houses of Congress Park
in search of that shadow, if only by that strange sense,

that sense that we have
yet to give a name to.

That sense that guides us to up
and quit a job in a fit of rage,

or to kiss the right person at the wrong moment.
That sense that hovers over us as we lay awake in bed,

in the middlest moment
of the endless night.

It was that sense that led me there
to float above the porch lights,

and with the gut of my gut seek out
that shadow that came to visit me.

Beneath the lamplit trees there was
no shortage of wonderful shadows,

but it was a particular breed of haunting and whimsy
that called to me silently in the spaces between the trees,

a something that carried in its shape a foreign intimacy.
As I hovered over Seventh Avenue, a car swept by.

I latched on convicted as
it sped down the corridor,

at a speed beyond what is common
for the Seventh Avenue stretch.

The world buzzed by me, a
collection of fragmented moments
and the car rolled onward,

unflinchingly crashing into the blackest cat
to ever wander a street at night,

and the cat did not stop,
nor did the car I had held onto,

the night tore onward,
at the tail of the car driving to elsewhence,

I let go, staying there with the cat that lay dead in the street,

where there was no one and nothing
but us and timeless,

and I watched as that shadow that I had followed softly
surrounded its broken form, unbreathing at the intersection.

It was then I felt what the shadow I was after had been,
as I witnessed the intersection of haunting and whimsy,

when our souls are no longer
in the bodies we've moved through

with such a beautiful negligence
and such an ugly grace.

(MILKWEED) SONG

After e.e. cummings

                              (a

                              le
                              af
                              fa
                              ll
                              s)
                    & it may stay fallen

        the monarch   misses (the milkweed)

            (the milkweed) waits
                        in the windless night

                    we flap our wings
                       toward what we used to know
                    was there

                                we sing our seeds
                        into the night
                                    still windless

                                    and wait

FISHING

You don't have to throw away your arm
along with the line,

in fact,
it's best to hold onto yourself,

unless of course,

your self is not yourself,

then fling it out into the water
with an Italian gusto,
a real fuck-all of a gusto,
that's the gusto the world is always
thirsty for.

For a lot of us,
the hard part is the not doing,
the not biting your nails,
the not pulling the cork out
with your teeth
(your teeth,
which you're going to need
for the rest of your life),
the not going back,

that's where you stay,
watching your line
stock-still in the water
taunting you with its maybe.

It's going to call you names,
remind you how stupid and small
and uneventful you are,

it reminds you again
about that one thing
that happened to you in fifth grade,
that ugly incident that is vaulted
securely in your bank of shame,
that is exactly who you are,

says your line,
all bait and no spoils,

says your line,
which I'd like to remind you,
is not you.

Meanwhile,
that pain in your lower back,
which also is not you,

but it sure burns
like a bath too hot.

That pain
that comes to sing
a little ditty
called dying.

And you're all line
and bait and back pain
and no spoils.

You're fishing.

Looking up
from the dead water
a new light is born
painting in its wake
revealing the line
for what it is,

the very same line
that runs across your palm
frayed but continuous
from your first ever yesterday
until right now,

your palm,
holding tight
to your line
pulled taught.

It could be nothing.

But it could be something.

It could be
a house that you built
from a burnt down forest.

It could be
a slow dance
in a fast-food parking lot.

It could be
that balloon
you let slip from your palm
and off it went
into the ether
lost to playing with the planes
but now
on the end of your line
at the edge of the world
out of the muck
it's come home to you.

THE STAND OFF

    High noon

Two saguaros ten paces apart
    in the vastness

    still as cacti
standing facing   one another
    to an audience of buzzards
        the brush   the heat

    A crow counts down
    cawing   ten
            nine
      eight
           then five
    then back to ten

    a long pause

      ten again
  nine   three
    two   six

    the moon arrives
    hanging in the balance
    until she too tires of waiting
    and calls it
    a night

    The saguaros remain,

  nine   five

    two   eight,

caws the crow
here in the desert
(womb cradling
 so much death)
the saguaros know better
than to pull their pistols
aim
and fire

    They hold   their arms
      straight up   towards
the open sky–
              and surrender
                in reverence
    to one
    another

UNDER THE TREE, BENEATH THE EVERYTHING

We are still under the tree,
beneath the everything.

We are still holding hands
in my car on Colfax.

We are still on a porch
where there are no clocks,
just endless questions
of what will happen
when Jupiter goes away,
but Jupiter never goes away,
it just dances in the wings
of the stage,
the way our love dances
in the wings of the stage.

We are still running
to City Park on our lunch break
to prove that magnets work
over longer distances
than science could ever predict.

We are still crossing the big blue lake
of maybe,
holding our shoes in our hands.

We are still waking up
to each other.

We are still on a plane
to somewhere.

We carry our love
like a basket of fruit
that never goes bad,
it only goes gooder,
it only grows greener,
because we sing to it
on rainy days.

We are still in rainy days,
where your ocean dances
with Denver,

where the sun is a candle
between us,

where we sing our songs
to each other,

where we are younger all the time
growing older together.

We are still walking long
and wicked,
forever endeavoring
to find one another,
under the tree,
beneath the everything.

CATALOG OF FLOWERS

A flower on fire in an otherwise dark mind.

A flower like a thought, an epiphany.

A flower spread out in petals across a street,
trampled by tires and time.

A flower in black hair besides black pupils
that churn your bright colors back into you.

A dead flower in a jacket pocket.

A flower inside the mouth of a bird.

A flower in a drawer in a desk.

A flower among a dozen flowers
swept up into a hurricane like a refugee,
unaware where it will land but left with no choice
but to be lifted until the fall.

A flower pinned on a wall like a butterfly.

A flower once white smeared by smoke.

The flower that dies first.

The flower that lives last.

A flower that never was gifted.

A flower that lived its whole life unseen
by sunlight; unpicked,
loved, disregarded,
left to be.

A flower inside of a flower inside of a flower.

A flower sucked under the waves.

A flower floating in hot water.

A flower that sees itself in the mirror.

A flower like a country at war.

A flower in a bouquet in a peace parade.

A flower like the wrinkles between your fingers.

A flower inside of a human mouth.

A flower like strewn-out jazz momentum dissipated into wisps of smoke and blown caustic like a ticking time bomb left laughing in a hotel room.

A flower behind a counter that can't decide if it's bitter or sweet.

A flower that collects your rainwater.

A flower that whistles in the wind, a flower that decided not to.

A mean flower. A painted flower. A frozen flower.

A flower that comes to your window.

A flower tied to a balloon tied to the sky.

A flower that grows wild on the wrong side of a mountain.

A flower that hangs by the wrist from the rafters.

A flower like a church bell.

A flower like a hailstorm.

A flower the shape of Venezuela, the shape of clouds, the shape of thoughts, the shape of destruction,

of retribution, of justice, of conviction in the name of
eating itself.

A flower that folds into its own petals.

A flower that flicks at the spokes of a bike tire.

A flower that lives between sunlight and stained glass.

Menace flower. Death flower. Archaic flower.
Witch flower. Green flower. Smoke flower.
Hell flower. Heal flower. No flower.

A flower that blooms for its own shadow.

A flower that so desperately wants to be a flower,
so mesmerized by itself, by its weight,
by the ways in which the green leaves bend.

A flower that thinks it can swallow the sun,
and the flowers that lean in to watch what happens.

HOW TO MAKE
A LAKE

We dug a hole
and prayed for rain

out in the vastness
sweating our days
into a dream that seemed
to only dance in our arms
pressing sharply against
the earth

some walked away
in burning laughter—
the word "no"
stuck on their tongue
like some dumb
honeysuckle

some stayed here
in the empty
and took their clean fingers
into the dirty ground

like shovels before
shovels

like trust before
trust

like an absence
before rain

and we became
a choir of hands
in manic unison

searching below
for a god
that we're so often told
we'll find above

and it was days
days that resist
being named

days that fill our blood
like music fills a room

and in the night
we wept
for everything that
could have been something
but remained in nothing

those tears
came in congregation
to the belly of the hole
we hoped would be a lake

and they stayed there
as long as a collective memory

and then the rain
the rain came like a migration
of buffalo
pattering against the ground
swollen and ready
to hold

and we did not run

the world was new
and old and fury
and soul

we opened our mouths
and received the sky

NOT
After Big Thief

It's not the window
that glares across the way
like an old box television.

It's not the bird
that you yanked
from the hands of death.

It's not the gift,
the perfectly wound watch,
that you forgot
to deliver.

It's not the humming power,
nor the once was a river,
not the gun in the safe,
nor the hand that is itching,
not the twilight of humans
nor the birthday of anger.

It's not the wheel made of squares,
nor the road made of patience,
nor the hangnail of violence,
nor the moon watching all of this.

It's not the lingering feeling
that nothing has happened,
and we're all still in March
and we're hiding for nothing.

It's not the weight of that moon
in the hand of a child,

nor the sound of the sun
in the om of the belfry.

It's not the window you drew
on a flat piece of paper
nor the box that it's in
somewhere deep in the water.

ON GRIEF

You might send your body
to swallow rocks on the shore of an empty
lake, or drive in left turns forever around the same
block that never changes as much as
you command it to. You might sleep
through a week or a year or a month and your
body needs that sleep and still sleep
more. Take care of your grief.
Climb a tree and scream
out the name of what is gone into the wind.
The wind, which carries away the echo of what
you were certain would return to you, or perhaps
what never arrived to begin with. Grief
is a feral cat. Take care of it.
It comes home to you hungry,
or tired, or because it needs
your attention as much
as you need something in your lap
reminding you that gravity
is real. Grief is an empty chair. Grief is
a photo in a drawer that
may or may not be in the drawer
you open it, you close it,
you open it again. Every prayer
sounding the way it feels
to drive by a pair of dim headlights on the
margins of the backroad in
a snowstorm. Grief
is writing the same sentence
over and over and
nobody can see it is the same sentence
but you. Grief quietly asks you to
feed it and it asks this in the name

of the dream flower that never
seems to grow in the empty pot you just
can't take down from your
dusty windowsill. Grief deserves
to be in the room, dancing or throwing
a tantrum the size of life or just resting its eyes
for a few brief moments. Grief
quietly asks you
everyday: will you tell me a story,
even though it hurts?

NEW HORSE

This new horse
arrived in the mail
today.

I expected it to be uneasy
but I did not expect it to run
so rampantly through my
apartment.

I expected it to eat my food
but I did not expect it to eat
all of my flowers.

I expected it in my daytime
but I did not expect it to follow me
into my bedroom at night.

I chop onions in the kitchen
and it hovers over my shoulder.

We listen to Frank Sinatra records
on the early nights of winter.

I feed it apples
and it feeds me company.

And now time is new
and I'm forced to recognize
that this new horse is no longer new
and though he still is somewhat destructive
he is now more familiar than anything.

INVOLUTION

It is an inherent act of defiance
to come closer in an expanding universe.

It seems, my friends,
what we need in our late hour of humanity
is a desperately intentional and radiant
involution.

What bravery would it be
if we said no to everything that isn't
each other.

What audacity would we be made of
to be late to work
because we had not yet departed
from our play.

To trim the entanglement of our trespasses
into a story we could softly hold.

Let us make time to fold into one another,
to lean in to leaning in,

to hold each other's pain
like an interwoven blanket
clutched in our collective hands.

To wipe the warpaint
off of the face of the culture we've been told
is our culture,
and have the courage to paint nothing new
in its absence.

Can't you see?
The war has co-opted
our identity of surrender.

Do we not surrender
our singular hopes
to the communal dream?

Does the tree not surrender
its broken branches, untamed children,
to the ghost ether of the river
that we've all always known?

Do we not surrender
our existential squawking
to the patient hum
of the Earth?

Which sings to us
listen,

listen like the thunder
listens to the lightning,

listen like the hungry wolf
listens to the sanctified cracking
of the bones of the rabbit.

Listen,
as if it was the most measured movement
you'll ever teach your body.

Your body—
the sacred fruit of your soul
offered as you wish
into a resolute being,

a righteous work,
and then collapsed into itself;
not a structure buckling to a boom
but an echo surrendering to its sound.

Acknowledgments:

"Bravery" was previously published by Aurora & Blossoms.

"Catalog of Flowers" was previously published by The Rumen.

"Fishing" was previously published by Twenty Bellows.

"I Am Waiting for the War to End" was previously published by Tabula Rasa Review.

"Mathematics" was previously published by Marrow Magazine.

"New Horse" was previously published in Spit Poet Zine

"Owlhead" was previously published by Unleash Creatives.

"Sound Reverberated Off of Mountains" was previously published in *Hero Victim Villain* (Stubborn Mule Press) and also by Twenty Bellows.

"The Lake" and "i see you there in half lotus" were previously published by Beyond The Veil Press.

About the Author

Brice Maiurro is a poet and storyteller from Lakewood, Colorado. He is the author of *Stupid Flowers, Hero Victim Villain*, and *Clown Singing Opera*. He is the Founding Editor of South Broadway Press. In his free time, he enjoys being an amateur mycologist and apiarist. You can find more about him at: www.maiurro.co.

About the Press

MIDDLE CREEK PUBLISHING believes that responding to the world through art & literature—and sharing that response—is a vital part of being an artist.

MIDDLE CREEK PUBLISHING is a company seeking to make the world a better place through both the means and ends of publishing. We are publishers of quality literature in any genre from authors and artists, both seasoned and as-yet undervalued, with a great interest in works which may be considered to be, illuminate or embody any aspect of contemplative Human Ecology; defined as the relationship between humans and their natural, social, and built environments.

MIDDLE CREEK PUBLISHING's identification as a Human Ecology press is meant to clarify an aspect of the quality in the works we consider for publication, and is meant as a guide to those considering submitting work to us. Our interest is in publishing works illuminating the Human experience of connection to each other, our selves, and to the world we share—to include not only the natural environments, but those that are human constructs such as history, economics, and the social sphere as well—through words, art, story, poetry so that we may reconnect to our potential deeply and more consciously.

www.ingramcontent.com/pod-product-compliance
Lightning Source LLC
Chambersburg PA
CBHW062120080426
42734CB00012B/2927